The
Book of Brilliant
BUGS

Written by
Jess French

Illustrated by
Claire McElfatrick

DK | Penguin Random House

Author Jess French
Illustrator Claire McElfatrick
Senior editor Satu Hämeenaho-Fox
Project editor Clare Lloyd
Senior art editor Claire Patane
Designer Rachael Hare
Editorial assistant Becky Walsh
Americanizer Liz Searcy
US Senior Editor Shannon Beatty
Educational consultant Jenny Lane-Smith
Senior producer, pre-production Nikoleta Parasaki
Assistant pre-producer Abigail Maxwell
Producer Inderjit Bhullar
Jacket designer Claire Patane
Jacket coordinator Isobel Walsh
Project picture researcher Sakshi Saluja
Managing editor Penny Smith
Managing art editor Mabel Chan
Creative director Helen Senior
Publishing director Sarah Larter

First American Edition, 2020
Published in the United States by DK Publishing
1745 Broadway, 20th Floor, New York NY 10019

Text copyright © Dr Jess French 2020
Illustration copyright © Claire McElfatrick 2020
Layout and design copyright © Dorling Kindersley Limited 2020
DK, a Division of Penguin Random House LLC
23 24 25 10 9 8
022–315390–Mar/2020

A catalog record for this book is available
from the Library of Congress.
ISBN 978-1-4654-8982-1

DK books are available at special discounts when purchased in bulk
for sales promotions, premiums, fund-raising, or educational use.
For details, contact: DK Publishing Special Markets,
1745 Broadway, 20th Floor, New York NY 10019
SpecialSales@dk.com

Printed and bound in China

For the curious
www.dk.com

MIX
Paper | Supporting
responsible forestry
FSC™ C018179

This book was made with Forest
Stewardship Council™ certified
paper—one small step in DK's
commitment to a sustainable future.
For more information go to
www.dk.com/our-green-pledge

From remote mountaintops to busy cities, bugs are all around us.

We share our world with bugs, living side by side with them but often overlooking them.

Turn the pages of this book to discover just how important creepy-crawlies are.

CONTENTS

4   **What is a bug?**
6   Invertebrates
8   A world of bugs
10   Meet the family
12   Insect bodies
14   Wonderful wings
16   Eye spy

18   **Bugs and their relatives**
20   Insects
22   Spiders and scorpions
24   Millipedes and centipedes
26   Sea snails and sea slugs
28   Wood lice
30   Segmented worms

32   **Bug behavior**
34   Pollinators
36   Life cycle of a moth
38   Cleaning up
40   Working together
42   Bugs that glow
44   In disguise
46   Super senses
48   Bug defenses
50   Ant defenders

52   **Bug habitats**
54   Living underwater
56   Cave dwellers
58   Master builders
60   Burrowing bugs
62   Pirate bugs
64   Extreme environments

66   **Bugs and me**
68   Super store
70   Bug menu
72   Helping the planet
74   Bugs at risk
76   Helping bugs

78   Glossary and index
80   Acknowledgments

WHAT IS A BUG?

A bug is a tiny animal with a giant family. You'll find bugs just about everywhere on the planet, from towering mountains and dry deserts, to your own backyard.

While many people think of bugs as just insects, some of their close relatives—other creatures in the arthropod family—are also known as bugs. Their wider family contains lots more amazing relatives, too. Bugs come in many different shapes and sizes, but what links all of these creatures together is that none of them have backbones; they are all invertebrates.

Bugs and their relatives are some of the most important creatures on the planet. Without them, our world would look completely different, and many types of plants and animals would disappear altogether.

Let's get up close and personal with these tiny beasts...

Invertebrates

Bugs are invertebrates—animals that don't have backbones. Of all the animals on planet Earth, 97 percent of them are invertebrates—and there are more than a million different types!

All animals without backbones are invertebrates, but not all invertebrates are bugs.

Vertebrates are animals with backbones, including mammals, birds, fish, reptiles, and amphibians. They make up only around 3 percent of all the animals on Earth!

Vertebrates look big and powerful in comparison to invertebrates, but the truth is that without bugs and their close relatives, most vertebrates would become extinct!

A world of bugs

Bugs and their close relatives keep the world working as it should by recycling our garbage, providing food for other animals, and pollinating plants. They are very good at adapting to different environments and can be found all around the world.

Specially adapted bugs can survive even in tough environments like hot, dry deserts.

LIVING TOGETHER

Bugs can be very social creatures. While some bugs are happy to live on their own, many bugs help each other find food, build homes, scare off predators, and raise their young.

Millions of creepy-crawlies burrow beneath the soil, while others prefer to build underwater homes.

Bugs have been around for
millions of years—they were here
way before the dinosaurs!

There are many weird
and wonderful bugs
living in our oceans.

BUG BEHAVIOR

Bugs have special ways to
communicate with one another,
using catchy songs, and even
funky dance moves!

MEET THE FAMILY

The invertebrate family is enormous!

We split it into smaller families to help us understand it a little better. Some of the main groups of invertebrates are arthropods, worms, and mollusks, but sponges, corals, and starfish are also invertebrates!

Bark scorpion.

Whip spider

Golden orb-weaver spider

Arachnids

Arachnids have eight legs. Their bodies are made up of two parts, and they don't have antennae or wings. They also have highly specialized mouthparts for grabbing prey and chopping up food.

Tick

Mite

Desert blonde tarantula

Vinegarroon

ARTHROPODS

The biggest group of invertebrates is the arthropods. It's gigantic!

Of all animal species alive on Earth today, 85 percent are arthropods. And most arthropods are known as "bugs." Every arthropod has a skeleton on the outside of its body, jointed legs, and a body that is split into segments (sections). Four of the main groups of **arthropods** are **insects, arachnids, myriapods,** and **crustaceans.**

Honeybee

Cardinal beetle

Damselfly

Insects

Insects are by far the biggest group of arthropods. In fact, around 80 percent of all animals on Earth are insects! Insects have six legs, three segmented body parts, compound eyes, and a pair of twitchy antennae.

Stick insect

Ant

Atlas moth

Leaf insect

Katydid

Praying mantis

Crustaceans

Almost all crustaceans live in the water and are well adapted to aquatic life. Most people don't consider crustaceans to be bugs, but there is one small exception: wood lice. They are the only crustaceans to spend their entire lives on land and can often be found in gardens and woodlands.

Wood louse

Dungeness crab

American lobster

Myriapods

Like insects, myriapods have one pair of antennae, but instead of three body segments, they can have more than 100! Millipedes and centipedes, the most common myriapods, can have more legs than any other creature on the planet.

Dragon millipede

Pill millipede

Common centipede

Giant tiger centipede

MOLLUSKS

Oyster

Octopus

Garden slug

Mollusks are soft-bodied invertebrates. Most of these bug relatives have hard protective shells, and some have tickly tentacles! Lots of them live in the ocean, but some live on land.

Mussel

Gastropods

The biggest group of mollusks is the gastropods. They have muscular bodies, hundreds of small teeth, and sensory tentacles for seeing and feeling. Most gastropods have shells, but some, like slugs, don't.

Nudibranch sea slug

Sea snail

WORMS

Worms have long, thin bodies and no legs. Segmented worms, like earthworms, have long muscular bodies split up into segments. They are very good at burrowing and swimming. Flatworms are very basic creatures, which usually live as parasites in the bodies of other animals.

Earthworm

Red mangrove flatworm

Leech

11

Insect bodies

There are thousands of different types of insects, but **they all have six legs and three-part bodies.**

HEAD

THORAX

ABDOMEN

Antenna

Eye

Leg

Claw

Exoskeleton

Most insects have **a pair of feelers** (antennae) coming out of their heads. Antennae help bugs smell, touch, and taste.

Eyes
Insects can have simple or compound eyes. Compound eyes are made up of hundreds of tiny cells that are sensitive to light.

Legs
Insects have three pairs of legs with lots of joints. They have claws at the tips for clinging to surfaces.

Exoskeleton
Insects often have hard outer casings, called exoskeletons.

INSECT MOUTHS

BUTTERFLY
Proboscis
Butterflies have long, hollow tongues that are perfect for sucking up sweet nectar.

FLY
Sponging
Fly sponges suck up soft food and liquid—no chewing required!

BEETLE
Chewing
Powerful beetle jaws are strong enough to chomp through wood.

BEE
Chewing and lapping
Bees also use their mouthparts for making honeycomb.

MOSQUITO
Piercing and sucking
Their needlelike mouths can pierce through skin.

INSECT LEGS

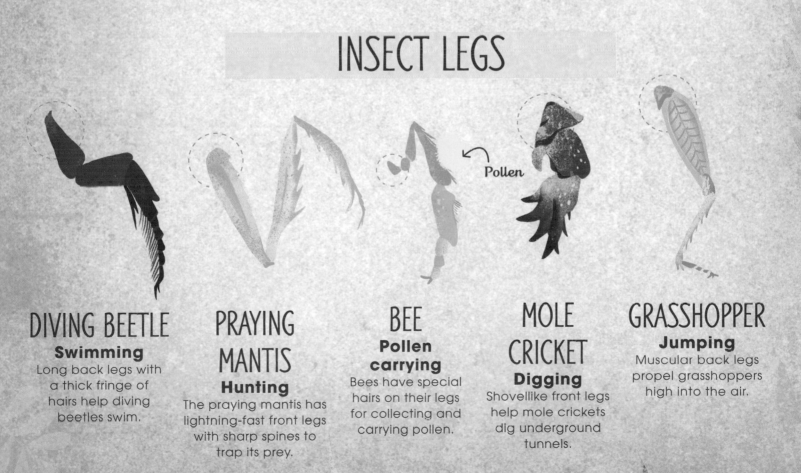

Pollen

DIVING BEETLE
Swimming
Long back legs with a thick fringe of hairs help diving beetles swim.

PRAYING MANTIS
Hunting
The praying mantis has lightning-fast front legs with sharp spines to trap its prey.

BEE
Pollen carrying
Bees have special hairs on their legs for collecting and carrying pollen.

MOLE CRICKET
Digging
Shovellike front legs help mole crickets dig underground tunnels.

GRASSHOPPER
Jumping
Muscular back legs propel grasshoppers high into the air.

Scaly wings

Butterfly wings are covered in thousands of tiny scales. Their wings can be brightly colored to attract mates or to warn predators to stay away.

Fly

Balancing act

A fly has one pair of large wings for flying and a tiny pair, called halteres, for balance.

Butterfly

Wonderful wings

Of all the flying animals, insects were the first to take to the skies. Millions of years before pterosaurs, birds, or bats, insects buzzed, fluttered, and flapped through the air.

Noisy wings

Crickets make chirping sounds by rubbing the upper and lower parts of their wings together.

Cricket

Built for speed

Reaching around 45 mph (72 kph), dragonflies are the fastest flying insects. They can fly forward, backward, up, and down. Each of their light and strong wings can be moved independently.

Bee

Some insects move their wings using muscles; others do it by changing the shape of their thorax.

Dragonfly

Hooked wings

Bees have tiny hooks that link their two sets of wings together, making it easier to move them.

Protected wings

Beetles have hard wing cases, called elytra, to keep their wings safe when they are not flying.

Stag beetle

15

Eye spy

Whether it's for **finding food, sensing light, or escaping attack,** eyesight is incredibly important for many bugs. Their eyes come in many different shapes and sizes. Some bugs have multiple eyes, each with a special function.

COMPOUND EYES

Insects and crustaceans have compound eyes, which are made up of lots of tiny lenses. They are usually **great at spotting movement** but not good at seeing details. Dragonflies and praying mantises have eyes that are very good at both.

Damselflies have two huge compound eyes that cover most of their head!

Simple eyes

Compound eye

Damselfly

Jumping spiders have eight simple eyes: four on the front of their faces and four on top of their heads. Their many eyes help them accurately judge distances, so they can leap right on top of their prey.

Jumping
spider

Have you ever tried to swat a fly? **Flies** can see movements up to five times faster than humans can, which is why they are so good at getting away from us.

Blue-
bottle
fly

SIMPLE EYES

Some arthropods have simple eyes instead of compound eyes. Some have both! Simple eyes are usually smaller than compound eyes and are **great at detecting changes in light**—helping bugs figure out what time of day it is.

Praying mantises see the world in 3-D, like people. This helps them snatch their prey out of the air as it zooms past.

Snails have eyes on the end of stalks, called tentacles. These bug relatives have poor eyesight, so they use a combination of feeling and looking to find their way.

Praying
mantis

Common
garden snail

BUGS AND THEIR RELATIVES

Insects, arachnids, and other creepy-crawlies are closely related to millions of other small creatures because they are all invertebrates. This broad group of animals includes arthropods, worms, and mollusks.

Although they belong to one big family, bugs and their relatives don't all look the same. From wriggling worms to scuttling spiders, they come in thousands of different forms.

The biggest group of invertebrates is the arthropods. This huge family includes insects, arachnids, myriapods, and crustaceans. And each of these families contains many fascinating members.

With so many weird and wonderful bug families to learn about, there is always something new to discover.

Insects

Insects make up the **biggest group of all the invertebrates**—in fact, of all the animals! There are more than **one million different types** of insects, split into 24 groups. These are some of the most well known...

Cockroach

COCKROACHES

These **scuttling bugs** are usually found cleaning up kitchens and living off human food scraps.

BEES, WASPS, AND ANTS

These little insects often live together in **big groups**. Some have stingers, which can inject a painful venom.

Orchid bee

Digger wasp

Ants

When searching for food, ants leave a **scented trail** for other ants to follow.

Leaf insect

Almost all insects hatch from eggs.

Dragonfly

DRAGONFLIES AND DAMSELFLIES

With two huge eyes and four beautiful wings, these insects are incredible **flying hunters**. They start their lives as nymphs living underwater.

Stick insect

STICK INSECTS AND LEAF INSECTS

Found mainly in tropical environments, these slow-moving bugs can **camouflage** to blend in with their surroundings.

Damselfly

Moth

Butterfly

BUTTERFLIES AND MOTHS

With their beautiful **fluttering wings**, butterflies and moths brighten up deserts, rain forests, mountains, and even our gardens!

PRAYING MANTISES

These **sneaky hunters** wait on plants and flowers before grabbing their prey in midair with specially adapted front legs.

Praying mantis

Nearly half of all insects are beetles!

Flower beetle

Mint leaf beetle

BEETLES

This enormous group of incredible insects lives all over the world. All beetles have hard **exoskeletons**.

Mosquito

Fly

FLIES

These small, soft-bodied insects have two large wings for flying and two small wings for balance, allowing them to **move quickly** through the air.

Earwig

EARWIGS

Usually found in cracks and crevices, earwigs often come out at **night**. They have long, thin bodies and sharp pincers.

Cricket

GRASSHOPPERS AND CRICKETS

These noisy leapers are often spotted hopping through **grasslands**. Locusts and katydids also belong to this group.

Shield bug

Cicada

Plant hopper

TRUE BUGS

Insects with **sucking mouthparts**, such as aphids, cicadas, planthoppers, and shield bugs, are known as "true bugs." They feed mostly on plants.

Aphid

Grasshopper

Spiders and scorpions

Arachnids are the hunters of the bug world. With eight legs and impressive mouthparts, they are perfectly designed to catch and kill their prey.

Many spiders make **silken webs** to catch their prey. They are the only arachnids that can make silk.

SPIDERS

About half of all arachnids are spiders. Most have sharp fangs, which they use to inject venom into their prey, but very few produce venom that is dangerous to humans.

Spiders can be very loving mothers, carrying their **egg sacs** with them to keep their unborn babies safe.

Cave spider

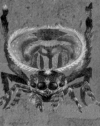

Australian peacock spider

Not only is the peacock spider bright and colorful, it also has some **super funky dance moves**, which it uses to show off and attract a mate.

European
garden
spider

Most spiders and scorpions make a toxic substance called "venom."

SCORPIONS

Like all arachnids, scorpions have eight legs. They also have big, grasping pincers that are actually part of their mouths! A scorpion's most famous feature is its long, arching tail, which it uses to sting and pin down its prey.

Scorpions have **stingers** on the tips of their tails to deliver venom.

Pincers allow scorpions to catch prey, scoop up water, and dance with mates.

Bark scorpion

Water spiders carry **air bubbles**, so they can breathe underwater.

Water spider

ARACHNIDS

The biggest group within the arachnid family is the spiders, but these other eight-legged creatures are just as fascinating.

Vinegarroon
This tropical arachnid protects itself by spraying acid out of its bottom.

Whip spider
Despite its name, this cave-dwelling arachnid is not a spider. It uses its extra-long legs to feel its way in the dark.

Mites and ticks
These bugs are called parasites, because they often live off the blood of other animals.

Daddy longlegs
Often confused with spiders, daddy longlegs are also known as harvestmen.

Giant brown millipede

Millipedes and centipedes

Members of the Myriapod family, like millipedes and centipedes, **can have up to 750 legs**! They use them for tunneling underground and chasing prey. Some centipedes even use their pointy legs to injure enemies.

Red millipede

Pill millipedes

MILLIPEDES

Millipedes are slow-moving creepy-crawlies. They use their many legs to tunnel, pushing their smooth, rounded bodies through soil and decaying vegetation. Most millipedes are vegetarians, feasting on dead plants and fallen leaves.

Pill millipede

Some millipedes, including the **African giant millipede**, roll into balls when they are frightened.

Dragon millipede

Bumblebee millipede

Millipedes have two pairs of short legs on each body segment.

Millipedes and centipedes are able to regrow lost legs!

Jungle centipede

CENTIPEDES

Centipedes are quick-footed hunters, capable of killing small vertebrates like lizards, snakes, and bats. They scuttle speedily in pursuit of their prey and can deliver venomous bites using their fang-like front legs.

Common centipede

Waterfall centipede

Centipedes have one pair of legs on each body segment.

Giant tiger centipede

MYRIAPODS

It isn't always easy to tell these strange creatures apart. Let's get to know them better.

Pill millipede
Sometimes confused with wood lice, pill millipedes (or "pillworms") have much shorter bodies than other millipedes.

Flat-backed millipede
As the name suggests, these millipedes have flattened bodies rather than rounded segments.

House centipede
Long-legged house centipedes can often be found scuttling around homes, eating cockroaches and other pests.

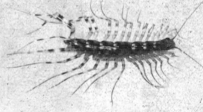

Scolopendra
These enormous tropical centipedes hunt birds, amphibians, and mammals.

Sea snails and sea slugs

You may already be familiar with land snails and slugs—the gastropods that live in our gardens. But some of their most fascinating relatives can be found **crawling along the seafloor and floating with the ocean currents.**

Magnified sea butterfly

The sea butterfly is a **tiny sea snail.** It uses its foot, which has two winglike lobes, to fly upside down through the water.

Many marine gastropods **breathe using gills.**

SEA SNAILS

With shells that are usually coiled into spirals, sea snails come in many different shapes, sizes, and colors.

Cone snail

The slow cone snail uses **lethal venom** to stop its prey from swimming away.

SEA SLUGS

The most common type of sea slug is the brightly colored nudibranch. It is often found in shallow tropical waters. Most nudibranchs have two hornlike tentacles and a fan of feathery gills.

Blue dragon nudibranch

Nudibranchs are often carnivores. They eat fish, algae, coral, and even other nudibranchs!

Dorid nudibranch

Sea bunny nudibranch

GASTROPODS

Most members of the gastropod family live underwater; only slugs and snails are found on land.

Slug
Soft-bodied slugs have no visible shells. They are often found in dark, moist places.

Snail
Snails have shells to protect their bodies. They can live in freshwater, seawater, and on land.

Limpets
The dome-shaped shells of limpets are usually seen clinging to rocky shores.

Abalones
Also known as sea-ears, these marine gastropods are hunted for their meat and beautiful shells.

Wood lice

Found all over the world, wood lice like to **make their homes in cool, damp places.** They particularly enjoy living under old, rotting logs. Wood lice are part of a family of creatures called crustaceans.

Wood lice are known by many names:
pill bug, roly-poly, sow bug, slater, butcher boy, coffin cutter, pea bug, cud worm, and cheesy bug.

Wood lice eat **fungi, rotting plants**, and even their own **poop!**

Wood lice babies

Wood lice mothers carry their delicate, bright white babies around in a pouch.

When they are frightened, **wood lice hide in crevices or curl up** into tight balls.

Although they live on land, wood lice **breathe through gills**—just like their underwater relatives.

Wood louse spider

Wherever you find wood lice, you will probably find this orange spider, which **hunts and eats wood lice**.

Common wood lice

Wood lice **shed old skin** as they grow.

CRUSTACEANS

Wood lice are the only crustaceans that can spend their whole lives outside of the water. Most crustaceans are sea animals.

Lobsters
Found on the ocean floor, lobsters use their powerful claws to snatch their prey.

Crabs
These clawed crustaceans can be seen walking sideways on seashores.

Barnacles
Sticky barnacles can glue themselves to boats, rocks, and even turtles and whales!

Krill
As they drift through the ocean, krill provide food for hundreds of other sea animals.

Leeches

Leech

These bloodsucking segmented worms feed on other animals and have been used in human medicine.

Segmented worms

Segmented worms like damp and wet environments, which is why we often see earthworms above ground when it rains. In addition to burrowing through soil, they can be found swimming in water, slithering through wet sand, and even tunneling through ice!

Earthworm

Earthworms

The most well-known of the segmented worms are earthworms. They mix and aerate (add oxygen to) soil, which helps plants grow.

They breathe oxygen

Earthworms don't have lungs.

WORMS

Segmented worms are one of three main groups of worms. Roundworms and flatworms are the two other groups.

Wriggle! Wriggle!
Segmented worms have two special sets of muscles, called circular and longitudinal muscles. They move along by squeezing each of these muscles in turn.

through their skin!

Giant blue earthworm

Giant blue earthworms
These huge Australian earthworms can grow to more than 10 ft (3 m) in length! They make gurgling sounds as they move.

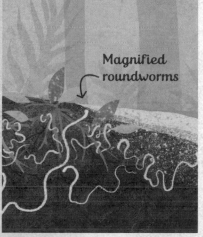

Magnified roundworms

Roundworms
Roundworms are found just about everywhere on Earth—including inside other animals' bodies! But they are very small, so you often need a microscope to see them.

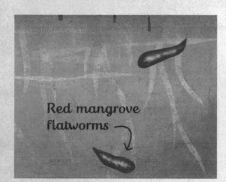

Red mangrove flatworms

Flatworms
Flatworms have soft bodies without any segments. Most of them are parasites (they live in or on other animals). The human tapeworm is a type of flatworm.

Honeybees begin their lives in cells within the beehive. They pass through four stages: egg, larva, pupa, and bee.

BUG BEHAVIOR

It's a great big world out there, and bugs are very small. But that doesn't stop them from being some of the world's greatest builders, soldiers, and masters of disguise.

Depending on where they live, every bug needs a different superpower. Some bugs are strong; others are sneaky. Some bugs use their skills to hide from predators; others use them to attract mates.

For some bugs, the secret lies in working together as a team. In big bug colonies, every bug has its own important job, and its survival depends on the actions of all the bugs around it.

Scientists are always learning new things about the strange and mysterious behavior of bugs.

Orchids

Orchid bee

Scented bugs
Male orchid bees, or euglossine bees, collect special oils from the orchids they visit and wear them as perfume. This is thought to help them attract mates.

Bees are important pollinators.

Pollinators

Flowers make a huge effort to attract insects, because insects help pollinate them. They use bright colors and strong smells to show off their nectar, a sugary liquid that many insects like to eat. When an insect lands on a flower to feed, it is dusted in powdery pollen. This pollen is then carried to new flowers, allowing them to produce seeds.

Bumblebee

Anicia checkerspot butterfly

Feeding time
Butterflies and moths have long, straw-like tongues, called proboscises, which they uncurl to suck up nectar from the flowers they visit.

Hummingbird hawk-moth

Proboscis

Fig wasp

Fig plant

There are around 900 different types of fig plant.

Pollination partners

Fig plants and fig wasps need each other to survive. Each fig plant is pollinated by its own special type of fig wasp. In return, the wasp will spend most of its life living snugly inside the fig it pollinated.

Cacao plants, used to make chocolate, are pollinated by midges. Without them, we wouldn't have any chocolate.

Midge

Cacao plant

Bee orchid

Bee orchid flowers look enough like female bees to trick male bees into visiting and pollinating them!

Flower beetle

Beetles have pollinated flowers for more than 150 million years.

Life cycle of a moth

Some insects have life cycles that are so unbelievable, they seem like magic. They start their lives looking one way and then turn into something completely different. **This process is called complete metamorphosis.**

EGG

The first stage of complete metamorphosis is the egg. After the moth lays its eggs, it usually takes less than two weeks for them to hatch.

Luna moth egg

Newly hatched caterpillar

Moths lay their eggs on leaves so that when the caterpillars hatch, they have plenty to eat.

Luna moth caterpillar

LARVA

The second stage of complete metamorphosis is the larva. Larvae love to eat! They need to grow big and strong before their huge transformation. In moths and butterflies, the larval stage is a caterpillar.

PUPA

The third stage of complete metamorphosis is the pupa. This is when the big transformation happens! The pupa cannot move, so it needs to be camouflaged to protect it from predators.

Moth pupa

Moth pupae are often wrapped in silk or buried underground to keep them safe.

Beetles, flies, butterflies, bees, wasps, and ants also undergo **complete metamorphosis**.

Once its wings have straightened out and dried, the adult moth flies off to find a mate.

When an adult moth first hatches, its wings are wet and crumpled.

Adult luna moth

ADULT

The fourth and final stage of complete metamorphosis is when the adult moth hatches out of the pupa. It now has wings and looks totally different. The adult moth's main purpose is to mate and lay eggs to continue the cycle.

Cleaning up

Animal poop may not look very appealing to us, but to dung beetles, it is **food and shelter**. Whether they roll it home or nest in it where it falls, one thing is certain: **dung beetles love poop.**

Dung beetles roll quickly to keep other sneaky dung beetles from **stealing their dung balls!**

Female dung beetles often hitch rides on top of dung balls, laying their eggs inside them.

A dung ball can weigh 50 times more than the beetle rolling it!

Spur

Rolling experts

Male dung beetles are well adapted to dung collection. Spurs on their strong back legs help them push the balls along. These incredibly strong dung beetles are called "rollers."

Dung beetle

Without dung beetles to clean up, fields and savannas could be overflowing with animal poop!

When they need to move quickly from place to place, dung beetles unfold their wings and buzz noisily through the air.

Buried treasure

Some dung beetles are known as "tunnelers." They use their powerful front legs to dig tunnels and bury their precious dung balls underground.

Smelly poop from omnivores (animals that eat plants and meat) is easier to find, but dung beetles **prefer the poop of herbivores** (plant eaters) like elephants, rhinos, sheep, and cows.

Home sweet home

While some dung beetles roll dung balls back to their nests, "dwellers" prefer to burrow into the dung heap and make themselves at home where they are.

Working together

Finding nectar, the sugary liquid inside flowers, is hard work. It can take a lot of flying to find the perfect patch of flowers. When honeybees find a particularly good source of nectar and pollen, they tell the rest of the colony exactly where to find it.

A colony is a group of insects that live together.

Foxglove flowers have nectar guides.

Honeybee

Bumblebee

Pollen basket

Finding food

Some flowers have special patterns on their petals called nectar guides. Bees use their excellent eyesight to follow these guides and discover the hidden nectar.

Carrying the goods

A bee has a special stomach for carrying nectar back to the hive. Some bees also have pollen baskets on their back legs to collect and transport pollen.

A bee colony's home is called a **hive**. This is where they transform **nectar into honey**.

Honeybees dancing in the hive

Tiny dancers

If there is a source of nectar close to the hive, the returning bees dance round and round in a circle. If flowers are farther away, bees do a detailed dance, called a waggle dance, which tells the worker bees exactly where to look.

The **angle** of the waggle dance shows the direction of the flowers.

The **length** of the waggle dance indicates how far away the flowers are.

Honeybee colonies consist of a queen, drones, and thousands of workers. Each bee has a specific job.

Honeybees build hexagonal honeycomb cells to store honey.

Beehive

Bumblebee drinking nectar

Bugs that glow

**Animals that create light
are called "bioluminescent."**
While a number of animals can do this,
including some ocean jellyfish, fireflies are
the only glowing creatures that can
fly. They dance through the air
in search of mates, lighting
up the forest with their
bioluminescence.

HOW THEY LIGHT UP

Fireflies make their glowing
light by mixing oxygen
and a fiery substance
called luciferin inside
their bodies.

Adult male
Photinus firefly

Photinus pyralis
("Big dipper")

Photinus ignitus
(ignited firefly)

Photinus consanguineus
(double cousin)

Photinus carolinus
(synchronous firefly)

Unique signals

Each species of firefly has its own pattern of lights. Some glow continuously, while others flicker and flash at regular intervals.

Dancing together

Synchronous fireflies can flash the same pattern at the same time. Millions of them come together in summer to put on a display.

A firefly's glow is the world's most efficient light. It loses almost zero energy as heat.

Finding a mate

Males and females use their lights to talk to each other and find mates.

43

In disguise

Bugs are small, making them seem like easy targets for predators. Luckily, over time, these masters of disguise have developed **cunning ways to hide in plain sight.**

Clearwing butterfly

Leaf insect

Dead leaf mantis

Almost invisible

Not content with only looking similar to their surroundings, some bugs are transparent (see-through). The clearwing butterfly has transparent wings, which means animals look straight through it.

Blending in

Camouflaged bugs can creep through their habitats undetected because they look like their surroundings. It makes it more difficult for attackers to find them.

Thorn bug

Being disguised as a leaf isn't always a good thing, though. Some **leaf insects** are mistaken for food by hungry herbivores!

The giant **swallowtail caterpillar** is often mistaken for bird poop!

Horsehead grasshopper

Groups of **thorn bugs** look like they are part of the plants or branches they sit on.

Fake eyes

Some bugs have eyespots that look like the eyes of bigger animals. Eyespots on bugs such as caterpillars and butterflies confuse and frighten predators and can deter birds and other potential attackers.

Eyespot

Owl butterfly

Pupa

The pupae of **owl butterflies** blend into their surroundings, helping them stay hidden and out of danger.

Hawk-moth caterpillar

Some **hawk-moth caterpillars** trick attackers into thinking they are harmful snakes.

Guess who?

For some bugs, just looking dangerous is enough to scare off attackers. Even harmless bugs use this trick to avoid becoming dinner.

Standing out

If you are poisonous, there's no need to hide. Nasty tasting or toxic bugs are often brightly colored to warn predators not to eat them.

Frangipani hornworm

HEARING

Excellent hearing helps bugs escape predators and find mates. They can often hear sounds at much higher pitches than we can.

Bat

Some **moths** can hear high-pitched bat ultrasound and fly away to avoid being eaten.

Moth

Mosquitoes choose their mates based on the sound of their buzzing wings.

Some bugs have ears in unexpected places. **Grasshoppers and katydids** have ears on their forelegs!

Earthworms don't have ears. These bug relatives detect animals moving nearby through vibrations.

Katydid

Ear

Super senses

Bugs and their relatives experience the world very differently from humans, but they use the same **five basic senses** to survive.

White-faced hornet

TASTE

We use our tongues for tasting, but bugs and their relatives can **use many different body parts**, including their feet!

Fruit fly

As soon as they land, flies use their feet to decide if the food is good or not.

Garden snail

Tentacle

Slugs and snails use their **tentacles** for tasting.

The white-faced hornet is a meat eater, but it is also drawn to sweet and sugary substances.

SMELL

Insects use their antennae to smell their surroundings. Moths' antennae are so sensitive that they can smell things many miles away.

Ants have a strong sense of smell, which they use to identify intruders in their colonies.

Antenna

Ants

Atlas moth

North American honeybee

SIGHT

Horsefly

Some bugs cannot see, while others can see much more than humans! Sight is particularly important for pollinators, which are drawn toward the tastiest plants by bright and colorful flowers.

Golden orb-weaver spider

Antenna

TOUCH

Tiny hairs cover the bodies of many bugs. These hairs are very sensitive to vibrations, helping bugs detect moving predators and prey.

Spiders can feel the smallest of **vibrations** in their webs.

American cockroach

Cockroaches have poor vision, so they use their **antennae** to feel their surroundings. They are also very **sensitive to vibrations**, which is why they are so skittish.

Water strider

Water striders can sense ripples on the water's surface.

Bug defenses

Despite their best efforts, **sometimes bugs come under attack.** And when they do, they protect themselves in a host of incredible ways.

Foul-tasting bubbles

Chemical defenses
Lots of bugs release nasty chemicals to ward off attackers. When disturbed, some moths release foul-tasting bubbles.

Earthworms secrete mucus, a slimy substance that helps them slide through soil and away from enemies.

Amerila moth

Earthworm

Noisemakers
Some cockroaches scare off their attackers by hissing. The loud noise is made by forcing air out through the breathing holes in the sides of their bodies.

Grasshopper

Losing legs
Some bugs, including grasshoppers, distract their attackers by dropping one of their legs! Many lucky bugs regrow lost legs after a few molts. A molt is when a bug sheds old skin to make way for new skin.

Madagascan hissing cockroach

Many bugs are protected by an exoskeleton, a hard outer layer that covers a bug's body.

Great escape

While some bugs "play dead" when they feel threatened, click beetles somersault high into the air and out of harm's way.

Click beetle

Saddleback caterpillar

Saddleback caterpillars are covered in venomous hairs.

Hazardous hair

Many caterpillars have hairs that secrete venom. The hairs cause painful itching and irritation if enemies come into contact with them.

Roll up, roll up!

Just like wood lice, cuckoo wasps can curl themselves into protective balls when they feel threatened.

Cuckoo wasp

Ant defenders

When wood ants feel their nest is threatened, they tuck their abdomens between their legs and spray out **jets of acid** at their attacker. Some sneaky birds get wood ants to spray their feathers on purpose to get rid of itchy mites.

Wood ant

Worker ants

Larvae

Wood ants often eat other bugs, such as caterpillars.

Nests can contain more than **300,000** ants.

Ants' nests have to stay at the right temperature for their babies to survive. So ants line their nests with grass and pine needles to keep them warm.

Wood ants sunbathe outside their nest. It helps warm their home when they return.

When baby ants (larvae) grow big enough, they wrap up in silken cocoons.

Workers bring food to their queen.

Almost all of the ants in the nest are female workers. They take care of the baby ants.

Ant royalty

Some wood ant nests have only one queen, but sometimes they join together to form huge nests with many queens. The queen's only role is to lay eggs.

Queen ant

Eggs

BUG HABITATS

Bugs are everywhere! Wherever you are in the world, you are sure to have some bug neighbors living close by.

Millions of years ago, the first bugs lived in the ocean. Now they have spread all over the planet. They can be found in the sky, burrowing underground, and in many places in between.

Bugs can survive in the toughest of places. From hot, dry deserts, to icy mountain peaks, bugs are experts at adapting to their environments. Some bugs even take over the homes of other bugs and animals!

Read on to discover beautiful and bizarre bug habitats...

Monarch butterflies avoid cold North American winters by making long journeys to warm Mexican woodlands. Once there, they spend months sleeping in clusters on trees.

Living underwater

Some invertebrates live their whole lives underwater. With no air to breathe, and hungry fish around every corner, these ingenious bugs have evolved **fascinating ways to survive in their underwater world.**

Adult mayfly

Whirligig beetles

Mayfly nymph

Breathing underwater

Some bugs, such as mayfly nymphs, have evolved gills to extract oxygen from the water. But other underwater bugs still need to get their oxygen from the air.

Underwater explorers

Underwater bugs move through their watery ecosystem in many different ways. Some swim through the water using their legs as paddles; others clamber about on rocks and plants. Some can even skate across the water's surface!

Diving beetles carry bubbles of air attached to their bodies.

Diving beetle

Mayfly

Dragonfly

Some bugs spend part of their life underwater and part of it flying through the air!

Water striders

Back swimmers use their oar-like legs to propel themselves jerkily through the water.

Back swimmer

Dragonfly nymph

Leaving home

Some dragonflies spend many years underwater as dragonfly nymphs before hatching into adult dragonflies. They shoot through the water by releasing bubbles from their bottoms!

Water scorpions use their long tails as snorkels, allowing them to stay under the water while breathing air from above the surface.

Apple snails produce layers of mucus to glide along rocks and vegetation.

Apple snail

Cave dwellers

Caves are dark, wet, and still. The bugs that live in them are **specially adapted to help them survive these unique conditions.** They are often blind and colorless, but some have extra-special senses.

Animals that have adapted to life in caves are called troglobites.

Cave millipede

Cave millipede
Like many cave bugs, cave millipedes look white in color. There's no need for them to blend into their dark habitat because cave-dwelling predators can't see them.

Whip spider

Whip spider
A whip spider's long, thin front legs are used for sensing. By gently touching its surroundings, a whip spider can build a picture of its pitch-black world and scuttle around, catching smaller bugs in its enormous jaws.

New Zealand
glowworms

New Zealand glowworm

The New Zealand glowworm is also known as a
"fungus gnat." In its larval stage, this small,
maggot-like creature hangs from the roof of its cave
in a silken hammock and dangles a trail of mucus to
catch its prey. When the maggot's tail shines, the
sticky fishing line lights up like a Christmas tree.
Prey is drawn to the spectacular glow.

Cave
snail

Cave snail

These bug
relatives often
have translucent
shells. Light passes
through them, giving
them a ghostly
appearance.

Cave crickets

Cave crickets spend their
days sleeping inside
caves and their nights
hunting for food in the
world outside.

Cave cricket

Cricket poop
provides food
for many
cave bugs!

Narrow-necked
blind cave beetle

Narrow-necked blind cave beetle

This beetle was one of the first cave species
discovered. It cannot see, so it avoids danger by
feeling its way around using its legs and antennae.

Master builders

Made from saliva, poop, and clay, termite mounds are incredible structures that can take a termite colony many years to build. The oldest termite mounds have been around since the time of the ancient Egyptians—and they are every bit as fascinating as the pyramids!

Cubitermes termites make **mushroom-shaped mounds.**

Hungry **anteaters** use their long, sticky tongues to scoop up termites from inside mounds.

Home invasion

Many animals actually steal the incredible mounds. Ants, bees, lizards, and parrots have all lived in termite mounds!

The **biggest termite mounds** are over 20 feet (6 meters) tall!

Some **birds nest in termite mounds.**

Chimneys and tubes allow air to flow in and out of the mound, maintaining a **constant temperature.**

Chimney

Worker

Termite mounds come in **many shapes and sizes.**

Hard at work

Each termite has a different job. Male and female termite workers are responsible for building and maintaining the nest, which can be home to over one million of their brothers and sisters.

Only reproductive termites have wings. Their job is to fly off and start new colonies.

Inside the mound, a maze of **tunnels** leads to rooms.

Queen

Termite larvae

The enormous **termite queen** can lay thousands of eggs every day, which hatch into babies, called nymphs.

Headlight beetle larvae

Headlight beetle larvae burrow into termite mounds and release a green glow. The bright green lights lure their prey to them.

Soldier termites defend **the mound** against intruders using their armored heads.

Life cycle

While ants, bees, and wasps all go through four distinct life stages of egg, larva, pupa, and adult, termites do not. When they hatch, baby termites look like tiny versions of the adults.

Although termites seem similar to ants, they are actually more **closely related to cockroaches.**

Soldier

Many bugs build their homes beneath our feet and spend their days scurrying through networks of underground tunnels.

Female mole crickets hear the loud chirping sounds and are enticed into the chamber.

Mole crickets
During the mating season, male mole crickets dig special sound chambers, which increase the volume of their songs.

Powerful legs are essential for digging.

A male mole cricket chirps inside his sound chamber.

Mole crickets spend most of their lives in networks of underground tunnels.

The **pupae** of many bugs live underground.

Pupa

Burrowing bugs

Many invertebrates live and spend time hidden underground. They might not wear hard hats, but these bugs can dig holes as well as any construction worker!

Ant lion larvae

Ant lion larvae dig funnel-shaped craters in soft sand, then lie in wait at the bottom. When an ant tumbles into the trap, they flick grains of sand at their victim until it falls into their waiting jaws.

Ant lion larvae eventually turn into ant lions, which look a little like damselflies.

Ant lion larvae have huge jaws as big as their heads!

Trap-door spiders

These spiders live in silk-lined tunnels, which they dig with their mouths. They sit waiting behind doors made of silk, then pounce on unsuspecting bugs as they pass by.

Female trap-door spiders can spend their whole lives inside their tunnels, making them wider as they grow.

Digger wasps

The solitary digger wasp lays each of her eggs in its own underground nest, which she digs using spiny brushes on her legs. Before sealing each hole, she pops in a paralyzed bug for her baby to feed on when it hatches.

Digger wasp

Spiny brushes

Pirate bugs

Plastic ahoy! Piles of waste in the oceans are bad news for the environment. But there is one tiny creature that is making its home on our plastic junk: the sea skater.

Life at sea

Sea skaters spend their entire lives on the open ocean. They are the only insects that are able to **survive** the big waves of cold, salty water.

Sea skater

Sea skaters have been found living on The Great Pacific Garbage Patch—an enormous area of waste floating in the middle of the ocean.

Future danger

Too many sea skaters upsets the balance of the ocean's ecosystem. They eat the plankton that other creatures, such as whales, depend on for survival.

Magnified plankton

Before the arrival of plastic, sea skaters laid their eggs on feathers and shells.

Sea skaters stay afloat using tiny bubbles that stick to the hairs on their six legs.

Eggs

63

Extreme environments

From freezing glaciers to scorching deserts, and from mountain peaks to the depths of the ocean, **bugs and their close relatives can survive almost anywhere!**

Fog-basking beetles collect the morning fog on their bodies, then do headstands to drip the liquid into their mouths to drink it.

Over many years, layers of fallen snow are compressed and turned to ice, forming glaciers. Tiny **ice worms** are able to wriggle their way through the cracks in glaciers and eat the algae that grows there.

Ice bugs are so well adapted to the cold that just holding them in your warm hands could kill them.

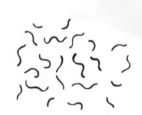

Flic-flac spiders cartwheel across the sand to escape danger.

Woolly bear caterpillars have antifreeze in their blood to stop the water in their bodies from turning into ice.

Despite their name, **sun spiders** are not actually spiders but ferocious arachnids that can take down venomous bugs like centipedes and scorpions. They avoid the hot desert sun by hunting at night.

TUNDRA
In a land full of **snow and ice**, where very few plants grow, bugs must cope in the harsh, **freezing winters**.

DESERT
Hot, dry climates make deserts one of the most challenging habitats for creepy-crawlies to survive.

Arctic bumblebees have thicker hair than their southern cousins, which allows them to withstand the cold.

Giant tube worms rely on bacteria to survive. They can grow to over 6 feet (1.8 meters) tall.

Snow fleas have special springlike body parts to help them hop through the snow.

Himalayan jumping spiders live on some of the highest mountains in the world, including Mount Everest.

These bug relatives are called **yeti crabs**. They collect bacteria on their bristly arms.

Deep-sea mussels thrive in the sulfurous water produced by the vents.

MOUNTAINS

High up in the mountains, bugs must survive with **little air and food** and withstand freezing cold temperatures.

HYDROTHERMAL VENTS

Openings on the ocean floor spurt out boiling hot seawater. **Bacteria** living in these vents feed almost all deep-sea life.

BUGS AND ME

For millions of years, bugs have lived and thrived on planet Earth. But since humans have been around, life has changed for just about every type of animal—bugs included.

The number of bugs is changing. Some species of bugs have increased in number, often as a result of human activity. But other bug populations have decreased, and some bug species are in danger of disappearing completely.

If we treat the environment kindly, bugs and humans can live in harmony for many years to come. Whenever we use, eat, or farm bugs, we must do so in a responsible, respectful, and sustainable way.

Most of all, we must remember that even though bugs are small, they are very important to our planet, so we must do all we can to protect them.

A jar of **peacock butterfly caterpillars**. Collecting bugs can be a great way to learn more about them, but always remember to put them back where you found them after you've finished.

Super store

SPIDERS

Spider silk

Spider silk is tough, strong, and very light. It has been used to make cloth and even violin strings, but it is very difficult to extract in large quantities, so spider silk is not often used by people.

OYSTERS

OPEN

Pearls

Some mollusks, such as oysters and mussels, produce pearls when things enter their shells that should not be there. Pearls can be used in jewelry.

SILKWORMS

Silk

Most of the silk we use comes from the cocoons of mulberry silkworms.

For more than 5,000 years, the cocoons of mulberry silkworms have been used to produce high-quality fabric items.

You won't bee-lieve the materials bugs and their relatives can produce. Thousands of years ago, people realized how useful bug-made products could be and started to farm bugs. Bug-made goods can still be found all over the world.

BEES

Honey
Humans first collected honey from wild bees around 10,000 years ago. Now, bee farming and honey production are big business.

Beeswax
Honeybee workers make a special wax to build honeycomb. We use it in candles and varnish.

Royal jelly
Bees make royal jelly to feed their babies and their queen. We use it in face creams.

INSECTS

Food coloring
Some red food dyes are made of ground-up scale insects from South America.

Venom
Venom might sound deadly, but in medicine it can be helpful. Bee and ant venoms are used to treat swollen joints and damaged skin.

PROBLEMS

Think twice
Bugs make lots of useful materials, but the way we harvest and process these products, including silk and dye, can be cruel. Silkworm pupae will die when their cocoons are destroyed to make silk, and many scale insects must be killed for humans to make just a small amount of dye. It is important to think about this before buying products made from bug materials.

Bug menu

People all over the world have been crunching on crawly critters since the very first human civilizations. Roughly one-quarter of people around the world still eat bugs, and there are more than 2,000 different types for them to choose from! In the future, bug grub could become one of the main sources of protein for our growing population.

APPETIZER

Mopane worms

Boiled and sun dried, mopane caterpillars are high in iron, magnesium, and zinc.

Ants

Zingy lemon ants from the Amazon rain forest refresh the mouth during meals.

Tarantulas

Deep-fried spiders are a common roadside snack in Cambodia.

Stick insects

Not a taste for everyone, stick insects have about as much flavor as a twig.

Escamoles

Also known as "insect caviar," these Mexican ant larvae taste like smooth and buttery cream cheese.

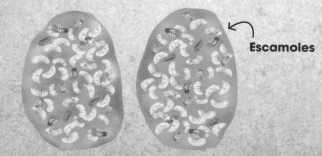

Escamoles

MAIN COURSE

Cockroaches

When fed fruit and vegetables, cockroaches are full of healthy vitamins.

Cockroaches

Termites

Fire-baked termites are dripping with fat and are a great source of protein, too.

Locusts

Usually fried or boiled into a broth, locusts have a slightly sweet taste.

Giant water bugs

Favorites across Thailand and Vietnam, giant water bugs taste like fishy scrambled eggs.

Fat-bottomed ants

A delicacy in Colombia, fat-bottomed ants have a strong salty flavor.

← Fat-bottomed ants

DESSERT

Stinkbugs

Don't be put off by their nasty smell; when cooked, stinkbugs taste like apples!

Aphids

Full of sugary sap, a fluid found in plants, aphids can be blended to make syrup.

Cicadas

These long-winged insects are often cooked with buttermilk. They taste smooth and nutty.

Honey ants

Honey ants are perfect sprinkled over ice cream. Their grape-like abdomens are bursting with sweet, warm liquid.

It is important that the bugs we eat are not endangered and that they are farmed responsibly.

CHEF'S SPECIALS

Kunga cake
A heavy cake packed with millions of squashed midges, kunga cake can be eaten on its own or used to add flavor to other dishes.

Casu marzu
Avoid this stinky, maggot-infested cheese. Eating it could harm the human body, so it's now illegal!

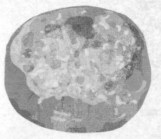

Witchetty grubs
When eaten raw, this bug's soft flesh has an almond flavor.

Chapulines
In Mexico, chapulines (grasshoppers) are roasted with lime, garlic, and salt and served on a corn tortilla.

Ant soup
In some parts of Asia, ants or ant eggs can add a sour flavor to spicy soup.

Mealworm quiche
When sprinkled on a quiche, mealworms give a nutty flavor and add a bit of a crunch!

Helping the planet

Many people think of bugs as pests, but in reality most of them are very helpful. In fact, **without bugs and their relatives, life on Earth would be completely different.** They are vital to our survival and the survival of the planet. Without these little heroes, the world as we know it would not exist.

Important pollinators

Imagine if there were no bugs to pollinate fruit and vegetables. Without bugs, a third of our crop plants and countless wild plants would disappear.

Robin eating an earthworm

The food chain

They might be tiny, but bugs and their relatives have a hugely important role at the beginning of the food chain. They are food for countless amphibians, birds, mammals, and reptiles.

In the delicate balance of nature, every creature plays its own important role.

Pest controllers

Predatory bugs keep many pest species under control by eating them, so that they don't destroy our crops.

Ladybug eating an aphid

Recycling enthusiasts

Nature's cleanup crew takes waste materials and reuses them for food. Dead animals, plants, and poop would become a real problem without bugs and their relatives.

Pill millipede feeding on rotting wood

Nature's gardeners

Below ground, bugs and their relatives prepare the perfect soil to help plants grow. Their poop acts as a fertilizer, and they make tunnels that allow water and air to reach growing plant roots.

Moths are drawn to unnatural sources of light.

Bugs at risk

All over the world, bugs are rapidly disappearing. This is mostly because of changes that humans have made to the planet. If we don't alter our behavior, they will vanish altogether.

Many bugs use natural light from the Sun and Moon to navigate and tell time. Artificial light confuses them, drawing them to the wrong places.

Climate change

Rising global temperatures and changing weather patterns affect the growth of plants and flowers. Sometimes this means that food for bugs is not available in the right place at the right time. If bugs can't find the food they need to survive, then the animals that eat bugs are at risk, too.

Habitat loss

As cities grow, natural spaces are lost, and forests are cut down. There are fewer and fewer places for bugs to live and feed.

Paradise lost

Gardens were once bug paradises. But as people put up more fences, tidy up their lawns, and put down plastic sheets and concrete, it is harder than ever for bugs to survive alongside people.

Chemicals are sprayed on farming land by special aircraft.

Harmful chemicals

Pesticides, including insecticides, herbicides, and fungicides, are chemicals used by farmers to keep their crops free of pests, weeds, and diseases. But they can kill the helpful bugs as well as the pests and are particularly harmful to bees.

Helping bugs

Bugs deserve our love and care. After all, they work hard to keep our planet in tip-top condition. Help them by building them a cozy new home.

BUILD A BUG HOTEL

Make space outside for your very own bug hotel—it's a great way to help bugs and recycle yard waste. Whether it's big or small, bugs will welcome a safe place to stay.

Fill a dish with pebbles, and add water—your guests might like a drink!

Ask an adult to help you lift heavy materials and build a stable hotel.

Collect

Gather materials for your bug hotel. Almost anything can serve as a home for bugs, but natural materials are best. Look for rotting branches, bark, twigs, pinecones, dry leaves, bamboo canes, logs, hay, and straw—the list of things you can use is endless!

Build

Look outside for the perfect place to build your hotel on flat ground. Space bricks evenly on the ground, then stack some old wooden pallets on top. Build carefully—you don't want your hotel to fall over!

Some bugs will pop into your hotel for a short visit, while others may choose to hibernate there during the cold winter months.

Fill

Get creative, and fill the gaps between your pallets. Start by adding larger materials like pots and branches, then gradually fill smaller spaces with things like pinecones and hollow plant stems. You can use straw and cut grass to fill very tiny gaps.

Decorate

Add the finishing touches to your hotel. Make a sign, and plant nectar-rich flowers like daisies nearby—they're the perfect treat for bees and other pollinating guests. Then sit back, and watch your tiny friends move in.

Glossary

ABDOMEN
The rear section of an insect's body.

ANTENNAE
A pair of feelers located near the front of an insect's head.

ARACHNID
An arthropod with eight legs and two body segments, such as spiders, scorpions, and mites.

ARTHROPOD
An invertebrate with jointed legs, a segmented body, and a hard outer skeleton, such as insects, arachnids, and myriapods.

BIOLUMINESCENCE
A chemical reaction that causes an animal to produce light.

CAMOUFLAGE
Colors, patterns, or shapes that help bugs blend into their surroundings.

COCOON
A silk case made by the larvae of many insects in which they pupate (become pupae).

COLONY
A group of animals, all of the same species, which live together.

COMPOUND EYES
Eyes that are made up of lots of tiny lenses. Can be found in insects and some crustaceans.

CRUSTACEAN
A type of arthropod which is usually aquatic and breathes through gills, such as lobsters and shrimp.

EXOSKELETON
A hard, outer skeleton that surrounds an arthropod's body, giving it shape and protection.

GASTROPOD
The biggest group of mollusks, these soft-bodied creatures have tentacles and hundreds of teeth.

HABITAT
The natural home of plants or animals, such as a forest, meadow, or rain forest.

INSECT
An arthropod with three body parts and six legs.

INVERTEBRATE
An animal without a backbone.

LARVA
A young insect that is at the second stage of complete metamorphosis.

METAMORPHOSIS
The process by which an animal changes from its young form to an adult form in stages.

MOLLUSK
A small, soft-bodied invertebrate, such as a slug or snail. Most have shells. The most common mollusks are gastropods.

MYRIAPOD
A type of arthropod with many legs, such as a centipede or millipede.

NECTAR
The sugary liquid made by flowers to attract insects.

NYMPH
An insect which is at an early stage of incomplete metamorphosis

OXYGEN
A gas in the air that all animals need to live.

PARASITE
An animal that lives on or inside the body of another species, known as the host. It harms the host but rarely kills it.

PEST
A harmful animal that attacks or destroys things, including crops.

POLLEN
The tiny grains that combine with a plant's eggs, so it can make seeds.

POLLINATION
When tiny grains of pollen fertilize female plants in order to produce seeds and grow new plants.

PREDATOR
An animal that hunts other animals for food.

PREY
An animal that is hunted for food by other animals.

PUPA
An insect at the third stage of complete metamorphosis, between larva and adult.

REPRODUCTION
When plants or animals make young.

SCAVENGER
An animal that feeds on dead animals, plants, and garbage.

SPECIES
Groups of animals or plants with shared characteristics.

THORAX
The middle part of an insect's body.

VENOM
A harmful or toxic substance injected by an animal or plant.

VERTEBRATE
An animal with a backbone.

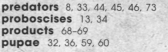

Index

abalones 27
acid 50
antennae 10, 11, 12, 47
ant lions 61
ants 10, 20, 37, 47, 50–51, 59, 70, 71
aphids 71, 73
arachnids 10, 19, 22–23
arthropods 5, 10, 19

back swimmers 55
bees 10, 13, 15, 20, 32, 34, 37, 54, 59, 69
beetles 10, 13, 15, 21, 35, 37, 49, 57
bioluminescence 42–43
bodies 12–13
bug hotels 76–77
bumblebees 34, 40, 41, 65
burrows 8, 60–61
butterflies 13, 14, 21, 34, 37, 44, 45, 52–53

camouflage 20, 44–45
caterpillars 44, 45, 49, 64, 66–67
caves 56–57
centipedes 11, 25
chemicals 48, 75
cicadas 71
climate change 75
cockroaches 20, 47, 48, 70
cocoons 51, 68
colonies 8, 20, 33, 40–41, 47, 58–59
communication 9, 40, 41, 43, 60
compound eyes 10, 16
crabs 11, 29, 65
crickets 10, 13, 14, 21, 57
crustaceans 11, 19, 28–29

daddy longlegs 23
damselflies 10, 16, 20
defense 44–45, 48–49, 50
deserts 8, 64
digger wasps 61
dragonflies 15, 16, 20, 55
dung beetles 38–39

earthworms 11, 30, 46, 48
earwigs 21
eggs 20, 22, 32, 36, 37, 59
elytra 15
exoskeleton 12, 21, 49
extinctions 7, 74
eyes 12, 16–17
eyespots 45

farming bugs 68–69, 71
fig wasps 35
fireflies 42–43
flatworms 11, 31
fleas 65
flies 13, 14, 17, 21, 37, 46
flowers 34–35, 40, 47
food, bugs as 70–71

food chain 72
fruit flies 46

gardens 75
gastropods 11, 26–27
gills 26, 54
glowworms 57
grasshoppers 13, 21, 46, 48, 71

habitats 44, 52–53, 75
hearing 46
hives 41
honey 41, 69
honeybees 10, 32, 40, 41
hornets 46
hydrothermal vents 65

insects 5, 10, 12–15, 19, 20–21
invertebrates 5, 6–7, 10–11, 19

jumping spiders 10, 17, 65

ladybugs 73
larvae 32, 36, 51, 59, 61
leaf insects 10, 20, 44
leeches 11, 30
legs 10, 11, 12, 13, 24–25, 48
life cycles 36–37, 59
light, artificial 74
limpets 27
lobsters 11, 29
locusts 70

mates 14, 22, 33, 34, 37, 42, 43, 46, 60
metamorphosis 36, 37
millipedes 11, 24, 25, 56
mites 10, 23
mole crickets 60
mollusks 11, 19
molting 48
mosquitoes 13, 46
moths 10, 21, 34, 36–37, 46, 47, 48
mountains 65
mouths 13
mussels 65
myriapods 11, 19, 24, 25

nectar 34, 40, 41
nests, ants 51
nudibranchs 11, 27
nymphs 54, 55, 59

oceans 9, 62–63
orchid bees 34
oysters 11, 69

parasites 11, 23, 31
pearls 69
pest control 73
pesticides 75
pincers 23
plastic waste 62–63
pollination 8, 34–35, 40–41, 47, 72
poop, animal 38, 39
praying mantises 10, 13, 16, 17, 21

predators 8, 33, 44, 45, 46, 73
proboscises 13, 34
products 68–69
pupae 32, 36, 59, 60

queens 41, 51, 59

roundworms 31

scolopendra 25
scorpions 10, 23
sea skaters 62–63
sea slugs 11, 27
sea snails 11, 26
segmented worms 11, 30–31
senses 46–47
shells 11, 18, 26–27, 57, 63, 69
sight 47
silk 22, 68
silkworms 68
simple eyes 17
slugs 11, 27
smell 47
snails 11, 17, 18, 27, 46, 55, 57
soil
spiders 10, 17, 19, 22–23, 47, 61, 64, 65, 68, 70
stick insects 10, 20, 70
stinkbugs 71

taste 46
tentacles 11, 17, 18, 27, 46
termites 58–59, 70
thorax 12, 15
thorn bugs 44
ticks 10, 23
touch 47
trap-door spiders 61
troglobites 56
true bugs 5, 21
tundra 64

underwater habitats 54

venom 22, 23, 25, 26, 45, 49, 69
vertebrates 7
vinegarroon 10, 23

waggle dance 41
wasps 20, 37, 49, 59, 61
waste 8, 38–39, 62–63, 73
water scorpions 55
water striders 47, 55
webs 22, 47
whip spider 10, 23, 56
wings 14–15, 37
wood ants 50–51
wood lice 11, 28–29, 49
workers 41, 51, 58
worms 11, 19, 30–31, 64, 65, 70

Acknowledgments

The publisher would like to thank the following people for their assistance:
Hélène Hilton for proofreading; Cécile Landau for editorial help; Polly Appleton and Eleanor Bates for design help; Dragana Puvacic for pre-production assistance; Helen Peters for the index; Gary Ombler for additional photography; and Tom Morse for CTS help. Many thanks to Martin French at BugzUK.

PICTURE CREDITS

The publisher would like to thank the following for their kind permission to reproduce their photographs:
Key: a=above; b=below/bottom; c=centre; f=far; l=left; r=right; t=top.

1 Dreamstime.com: Apisit Wilaijit (fbl). **2-3 Dreamstime.com:** Designprintck (Background). **4-5 123RF.com:** Mohd Hairul Fiza Musa. **5 Dreamstime.com:** Designprintck. **6 123RF.com:** sunshinesmile (cra/Butterfly, ca, tc, ca/Butterfly 1, cla, fclb, clb, cb, cr). **Dreamstime.com:** Alle (cra, cl). **7 123RF.com:** Panu Ruangjan / panuruangjan (ca). **8 Dorling Kindersley:** Peter Warren (fclb). **Dreamstime.com:** Tirrasa (clb/Ladybug); Svetlana Larina / Blair_witch (clb). **9 Dorling Kindersley:** Jerry Young (bl). **Dreamstime.com:** Fibobjects (clb/Daisy); Sarah2 (clb, tc). **PunchStock:** Corbis (clb/Butterfly). **10-11 Dorling Kindersley:** RHS Wisley (Pink Flowers). **10 Dorling Kindersley:** Gyuri Csoka Cyorgy (c); Jerry Young (cb). **Dreamstime.com:** Designprintck (l/ Background); Sarah2 (tc). **Fotolia:** Photomic (cb/Moth). **11 Dorling Kindersley:** Linda Pitkin (cr). **iStockphoto.com:** Mrfiza (br). **12 Dreamstime.com:** Cosmin Manci / Cosmin. **14 123RF.com:** Alexandr Pakhnyushchyy / alekss (cra); sunshinesmile (tl). **15 123RF.com:** Kriachko (b). **Dreamstime.com:** Alle (cl). **16 Dreamstime.com:** Razvan Cornel Constantin (b). **17 Dorling Kindersley:** Jerry Young (bl). **Dreamstime.com:** Cherdchai Chaivimol (tr); Kunchit Jantana (br). **18-19 123RF.com:** Vaclav Volrab. **19 Dorling Kindersley:** Jerry Young (bc). **Dreamstime.com:** Designprintck (Background). **20-21 Dreamstime.com:** Designprintck (Background). **20 Dorling Kindersley:** Jerry Young (bl). **21 123RF.com:** huandi (cl); Narupon Nimpaiboon (fclb); Eric Isselee (cb). **Alamy Stock Photo:** imageBROKER (clb, bc); Konstantin Nechaev (cra); VisualNarrative (cb/Green grocer). **Dreamstime.com:** Monypat7 (br). **22 123RF.com:** Marina Gloria Gallud Carbonell (b). **23 Dreamstime.com:** Designprintck (r/ Background); Isselee (tc). **24 Dorling Kindersley:** Stephen Oliver (t). **25 123RF.com:** Bonzami Emmanuelle / Scolopendra; Song Qiuju (crb). **Dreamstime.com:** Designprintck (r/Background). **26 123RF.com:** Ten Theeralerttham / rawangtak (br). **Alamy Stock Photo:** Blickwinkel (c). **Ardea:** Paulo Di Oliviera (cb). **Dorling Kindersley:** Linda Pitkin (b). **26-27 123RF.com:** Ten Theeralerttham / rawangtak (c). **27 Dorling Kindersley:** Holts Gems (c/Coral); Linda Pitkin (cb); Natural History Museum, London (cla). **Dreamstime.com:** Andamanse (bc); Designprintck (r/Background); Brad Calkins / Bradcalkins (cr). **Getty Images:** Antonio Camacho (c). **28-29 Dreamstime.com:** Sergei Razvodovskij / Snr (Leaves). **28 Dorling Kindersley:** Jerry Young (crb). **29 Dorling Kindersley:** Peter Warren (bl); Jerry Young (fclb, cb, cb/ Woodlouse). **Dreamstime.com:** Designprintck (r). **30 Dorling**

Kindersley: Thomas Marent (tc); Stephen Oliver (cl, clb). **31 Alamy Stock Photo:** Ephotocorp (cb). **Dreamstime.com:** Designprintck (r/Background). **32-33 Getty Images:** Paul Starosta. **33 Dreamstime.com:** Designprintck (Background). **34 Getty Images:** Buddy Mays (clb). **35 Dorling Kindersley:** Barrie Watts (ca); Tyler Christensen (ca/Fig wasp). **36 Alamy Stock Photo:** Papilio (clb). **SuperStock:** Animals Animals (cra, br). **37 Alamy Stock Photo:** Pixels of Nature (l). **Dreamstime.com:** Melinda Fawver (cra). **38 Dreamstime. com:** Cynoclub (cra). **naturepl.com:** Barry Mansell (c); MYN / Clay Bolt (crb). **39 123RF.com:** Pan Xunbin (cra). **Alamy Stock Photo:** Rolf Nussbaumer Photography (clb). **Dreamstime.com:** Neal Cooper (cb); Duncan Noakes (br). **40 123RF.com:** Elen1 (c); Oksana Tkachuk (bc); Peterwaters (ca). **40-41 Dreamstime.com:** Fibobjects (b). **41 123RF.com:** Oksana Tkachuk / ksena32 (cb, crb); Peterwaters (cra). **42 Dorling Kindersley:** NASA (t). **Getty Images:** James Jordan Photography (bc). **44 123RF.com:** ankorlight (tr); Tyler Fox (crb). **45 123RF.com:** Caritaliberato (bc). **Dorling Kindersley:** Natural History Museum (ca). **naturepl.com:** Mark Bowler (cb). **46 Dreamstime.com:** Bruce Macqueen / Lightwriter1949 (br); Roblan (clb/All flies). **47 123RF.com:** Andrey Pavlov (ca); Aukid Phumsirichat (cl). **Alamy Stock Photo:** Blickwinkel (tl); Katrina Brown / Tobkatrina (cra). **48 Alamy Stock Photo:** Avalon / Photoshot License (c). **Dreamstime.com:** Mr. Smith Chetanachan (bl); Michieldewit (cr); Monypat7 (crb). **49 Dreamstime.com:** Steve Byland (c). **Science Photo Library:** Claude Nuridsany & Marie Perennou (crb). **50 123RF.com:** Christian Mueringer (bl, clb); Sebastian Vervenne (tc). **Dreamstime.com:** Tirrasa (clb/Ladybug). **50-51 Dreamstime.com:** Vladimirdavydov (Ants). **51 123RF.com:** Christian Mueringer (cla, cr, crb, br). **Dreamstime.com:** Poravute Siriphiroon (bc); Tirrasa (cr/ Ladybug). **52-53 Alamy Stock Photo:** Brian Overcast. **53 Dreamstime.com:** Designprintck (Background); Jens Stolt / Jpsdk (crb). **54-55 123RF.com:** Pan Xunbin (ca). **54 Dorling Kindersley:** Peter Anderson (br); Natural History Museum, London (cla). **55 Dorling Kindersley:** Natural History Museum, London (t). **Dreamstime.com:** Cynoclub (cra); Pnwnature (c). **56-57 123RF.com:** Marina Gloria Gallud Carbonell (b/Background). **57 Dorling Kindersley:** Natural History Museum, London (cb, cr, crb). **Dreamstime. com:** Mark Eaton (br). **58 naturepl.com:** John Abbott (c, crb, tr, cra). **58-59 Dorling Kindersley:** Lynette Schimming (All). **59 123RF.com:** Werayut Nueathong (cb). **Dreamstime. com:** Apisit Wilaijit (br). **naturepl.com:** John Abbott (tl, bl, cla, cb, cra, tc). **60-61 Dreamstime.com:** Sergey Tolmachyov (b). **63 Dorling Kindersley:** Natural History Museum, London (clb). **64 123RF.com:** Charles Brutlag (clb). **Alamy Stock Photo:** Westend61 GmbH (cr); Ann and Steve Toon (ca). **naturepl.com:** Emanuele Biggi (cb/Camel spider); Nature Production (ca). **65 Alamy Stock Photo:** Nigel Cattlin (cb). **naturepl.com:** Gavin Maxwell (clb); David Shale (cb/Deepsea Yeti crab). **66-67 Getty Images:** Westend61. **67 Dreamstime.com:** Designprintck (Background). **68 123RF.com:** nito500 (clb/Flowers). **Alamy Stock Photo:** PhotoSpin,Inc (clb). **Dorling Kindersley:** Natural History Museum, London (fcr). **Dreamstime.com:** Fotofred (bl); Luanateutzi (cr). **69 123RF.com:** nito500 (crb); Peterwaters (br). **Dorling Kindersley:** Stephen Oliver (ca). **70 Dreamstime.com:** Monypat7 (tc). **72 Alamy Stock Photo:** Design Pics Inc (cb). **Dorling Kindersley:** Stephen Oliver (bl). **Dreamstime.com:** Brad Calkins / Bradcalkins (cr); Svetlana Larina / Blair_witch (cra). **73 Dreamstime.com:** Tirrasa (tr). **Fotolia:** Giuliano2022 (br); Eric Isselee (cb). **74 Dorling Kindersley:** Natural History Museum, London (cra, ca, ca/Scarlet Tiger, clb, crb, fcr, cr, ca/Green Silver-lines Moth, ca/Green Silver-lines Moth 1, cl). **Fotolia:** Photomic (cra/Giant Atlas Moth, cl/Giant Atlas Moth). **77 123RF.com:** nito500 (cb). **78-79 Dreamstime.com:** Designprintck (Background). **80 Dreamstime.com:** Designprintck (Background). **Cover images:** Front: **Alamy Stock Photo:** Panther

Media GmbH clb; **Dorling Kindersley:** Gyuri Csoka Cyorgy br, Ian Cuppleditch bl/ (Fagus), Ian Cuppleditch br/ (Fagus), Jerry Young cb, James Laswel tc, Natural History Museum, London bl; **Dreamstime.com:** Carlosphotos cra, Sarah2 fbr, Svetlana Larina / Blair_witch cla, Tirrasa bl/ (Ladybug), Tirrasa tl, Tirrasa cla/ (Ladybug); **PunchStock:** Corbis crb; Back: **Dorling Kindersley:** Gyuri Csoka Cyorgy cla, Ian Cuppleditch tl, Jerry Young cra, Jerry Young bc, James Laswel tc; **Dreamstime.com:** Carlosphotos clb, Svetlana Larina / Blair_witch cra/ (Butterfly), Tirrasa cr/ (Ladybug). **Endpaper images:** Front: **Dreamstime.com:** Tirrasa (All); Back: **Dreamstime.com:** Tirrasa (All).

All other images © Dorling Kindersley

ABOUT THE AUTHOR

Jess French is a nature lover who is passionate about bugs. When she's not helping animals as a vet, she's busy writing books about the natural world.

ABOUT THE ILLUSTRATOR

Claire McElfatrick is a freelance artist. She created illustrated greeting cards before working on children's books. Her hand-drawn and collaged illustrations for *The Magic & Mystery of Trees* and *The Book of Brilliant Bugs* are inspired by her home in rural England.